# She Did What She Could

# Study Guide

## Elisa Morgan

NAVPRESS
Discipleship Inside Out™

Discipleship Inside Out™

NavPress is the publishing ministry of The Navigators, an international Christian organization and leader in personal spiritual development. NavPress is committed to helping people grow spiritually and enjoy lives of meaning and hope through personal and group resources that are biblically rooted, culturally relevant, and highly practical.

**For a free catalog go to www.NavPress.com**
**or call 1.800.366.7788 in the United States or 1.800.839.4769 in Canada.**

# Contents

# She Did What She Could

## A relationship with Jesus results in a response.

*"I don't have an amazing story of a ministry I started, but the other day I was in the ninety-nine-cent store and an old man came up to me and asked if he could borrow a dollar to buy some food. I happened to have only one dollar in my wallet and gave it to him. And that phrase came to mind: 'She did what she could.' It wasn't much, but it was what I had at the time."*—JAIMIE

Begin by watching the "Message from Elisa" video clip from the SDWSC website (www.sdwsc.com).

## CONSIDER THIS

Do you see it? Do you see what she did in Mark 14:3-9?

> While he was in Bethany, reclining at the table in the home of Simon the Leper, a woman came with an alabaster jar of very expensive perfume, made of pure nard. She broke the jar and poured the perfume on his head.
>
> Some of those present were saying indignantly to one another, "Why this waste of perfume? It could have been sold for more than a year's wages and the money given to the poor." And they rebuked her harshly.
>
> "Leave her alone," said Jesus. "Why are you bothering her? She has done a beautiful thing to me. The poor you will always have with you, and you can help them any time you want. But you will not always have me. She did what she could. She poured perfume on my body beforehand to prepare for my burial. Truly I tell you, wherever the gospel is preached throughout the world, what she has done will also be told, in memory of her." (NIV)

Let's stop and ponder the first five words of verse 8.

*She*: God chose a girl. God chose a woman who acted on her love for him in response to his love for her. If this grabs your attention today, just imagine how God's choice sat with the crowd just after the crossroads of time between BC and AD, when women were little more than property. Slaves. Chattel. In fact, tradition held that each morning, Jewish males offered a blessing that thanked God for not making them Gentiles, slaves, or women.[1]

In choosing a girl, Jesus made a radical choice to make a point with incredible significance. No matter what we think of ourselves, God has chosen us to do things with amazing significance. Your giftedness, experience, and financial status have little bearing. Neither does your age or appearance. Jesus didn't choose a girl — Mary — by accident. He chose a girl on purpose. He paired her action with the gospel that would be preached through all generations. Jesus witnessed many wonderful and worshipful deeds by both men and women. He chose to make a big deal out of this one.

**Did**: She acted. She didn't just think about acting. She didn't act out of obligation. She didn't let others act for her. She didn't wait to be invited.[2]

*Doing* something is important. Simply moving into action is vital. But so is attitude. Mary offered her perfume genuinely, without regrets. Her action was not part of a reward system or a tally of deeds. Her action was intentional, not rash and last-minute. She didn't know the outcome, but that wasn't important. It's easy to have good ideas but much harder to act on them. Mary walked into a room of people, many who would not understand her intentions or her reasoning. She knew she was taking a risk. She also knew she was loved. Her action was in response to the love she'd been shown by Jesus.

**What**: She did *what* she could, not *all* she could. Rather than give this and that and then some more, only to eventually fall, spent, at his feet, she gave what she could and left it at that. Enough. A lot. Just right. She chose *what* she could and gave it ungrudgingly.[3]

Mary didn't empty her closet and cupboards. She didn't paint or write or draw. She didn't accompany her gift with beautiful singing or an inspiring dance. She could have, perhaps. She just simply and authentically did what she could. Her response came from her relationship with Jesus. This time she gave a lot. But that's not what

Jesus honored. He simply said, "She did a beautiful thing. She did what she could." He noticed that it was just what was needed at that particular moment.

**She**: She was a specific woman with a specific story who acted out of the particulars of her life. She acted because she knew she was loved and wanted to love back.[4]

Her story, her experiences, her possessions, her giftedness, her circle of friends. These were the particulars of her life. She looked around at what she had and gave from that. She didn't try to be someone she wasn't. She could have prepared an incredible meal, but that was Martha's gifting. She could have stood at the door and welcomed everyone and washed their feet, but that wasn't her calling. She was Mary and she had a special jar of nard. She had a love for Jesus because of the love he had given to her and her family. Not only had Jesus encouraged Mary, he had healed her father, discipled her sister, and raised her brother. So she did what she could in a way that demonstrated her love.

**Could**: She acted with what she had. Mary grabbed hold of what she possessed—what was within her reach, under her power, obedient to her control—and invested it. She did what she could with what she had to work with. She took the bottle of nard and made the most of it, right then and there.[5]

Mary didn't set out to save the world. She simply did what she could, what was within her reach at that given moment. She used the nard to anoint his body *before* he died. What's the point of all this? What's the significance of She Did What She Could (SDWSC)? A relationship with Jesus results in a response. When we *get* that we are loved by him, we are changed from the inside out. The transformation *inside* of us changes how we live *outside* of us. We put feet on our faith.

Take a look at the following chart and consider the application question corresponding to each of these five words: *she, did, what, she, could.*

*Mary of Bethany*

| She | Who was Mary in God's sight? *a girl sitter at his feet. tell us Jesus gets a response, acts* |
|---|---|
| Did | What did Mary do? *nowness to her action - got up & invested what she had —,* |
| What | What did Mary give? *Nard - gift - rose red oil substance spikenard of India 300 denarie Chanel 5 - alabaster container - neck w/ stopper carved. a lot expensive gift* |
| She | What was the significance of her gift? *out of a developing rel. character in contact w/ Jesus - transformed - would go at at his feet - touched Jesus in this moment, anointing body before burial - gave back to Jes gesture of love* |
| Could | What other options might Mary have had? *acted grabbed what she ha invested in public - anointing his body before his cros I believe He's messiah! Evangelical action* |

*Not all she could,*

*med Bro Laz. dies John 11.*

## CONTEMPLATE THIS

1. What do you think was most expensive for Mary — her perfume or the risk of giving it in a room of religious men in the day she lived?

2. What do you think changed for Mary as a result of her actions?

3. Why do you think Jesus chose a girl?

4. Explain what you think "A relationship with Jesus results in a response" means.

5. Why didn't one of the disciples do what Mary did?

6. Why do you think Jesus paired Mary's action with the telling of the gospel message?

7. What's the most interesting new idea for you from this lesson?

## INVESTIGATE THIS

Take a look at some other examples of biblical people who did what they could.

| Scripture | Who did what they could? | What did they do? | What was the result of their action? |
|---|---|---|---|
| John 6:1-13 | | | |
| Luke 21:1-4 | | | |
| 1 Samuel 17:32-50 | | | |
| Esther 4:6-17; 8:1-8 | | | |

8. How are each of these accounts alike?

9. What lessons can be learned by comparing these accounts to the account in Mark 14:3-9?

10. What biblical accounts show people doing what they could in small ways? In big ways?

11. How were these responses an outgrowth of each person's relationship with God?

Visit the SDWSC website and click on "Your SDWSC Stories" to read Chrissy's story.

## RESPOND TO THIS

12. What is a recent SDWSC example you've experienced?

13. What attitude comes with SDWSC thinking?

14. Where does your relationship with Jesus fit into the SDWSC equation?

15. How do your actions demonstrate your relationship with Jesus?

16. Does SDWSC thinking need to include doing both big and small, covert and overt?

End your time by praying for opportunities in the coming week to seize SDWSC moments.

## APPLY THIS

Using an index card, create a reminder for this week to put on a desktop, dashboard, fridge, etc. On one side write the letters "SDWSC." The other side should say, "A relationship with Jesus results in a response."

Commit to keeping the card in sight all week and bringing a story, written on an index card, to the next session.

Consider also posting your story on the SDWSC website (www.sdwsc.com).


Name

Date

My SDWSC Story

Judas betrayed for 30 denari
"Leave her alone" said Jesus. Poor you'll
have w/ you always, and if you can help them any
time you want! I tell you truth - you won't always
have one. Gospel = love lived out w/ action
what if I did what I could?
why don't I do what I could?
All in process...

Paid attention, a little at a time.

We spill over!

SDWSC - Before, she sat at my feet!
Sit at my feet w/ me.

Radical Transformation!

Letting God be the difference in our lives!

# Who Did What She Could and Why?

## Live loved.

*"Knowing that Jesus receives what I do for him, in response to his love for me, as 'a beautiful thing' is helping me keep doing what I could. And in doing so, I am finding out more and more what it means to live loved."*—CANDIE

Begin your time with a video clip. Visit the SDWSC website (www.sdwsc.com) and click on "Order the Book." Then click on the "This inspiring book . . ." video clip. If meeting with others, share the story you wrote this past week. Explain why that story was meaningful for you. Post your story on the storyboard.

---

A storyboard is a simple way to share your stories each week if you're doing the study in a group. It can be as simple as a cardboard "display board," a bulletin board in a hallway, or even a virtual storyboard on the church website for women to add their stories each week.

---

## CONSIDER THIS

There's more than one way to see what Mary did. Both Matthew 26:6-13 and John 12:1-8 record the same event:

> Jesus was in Bethany at the home of Simon, a man who had previously had leprosy. While he was eating, a woman came in with a beautiful alabaster jar of expensive perfume and poured it over his head.
>
> The disciples were indignant when they saw this. "What a waste!" they said. "It could have been sold for a high price and the money given to the poor."
>
> But Jesus, aware of this, replied, "Why criticize this woman for doing such a good thing to me? You will always have the poor among you, but you will not always have me.

She has poured this perfume on me to prepare my body for burial. I tell you the truth, wherever the Good News is preached throughout the world, this woman's deed will be remembered and discussed." (Matthew 26:6-13)

Six days before the Passover celebration began, Jesus arrived in Bethany, the home of Lazarus—the man he had raised from the dead. A dinner was prepared in Jesus' honor. Martha served, and Lazarus was among those who ate with him. Then Mary took a twelve-ounce jar of expensive perfume made from essence of nard, and she anointed Jesus' feet with it, wiping his feet with her hair. The house was filled with the fragrance.

But Judas Iscariot, the disciple who would soon betray him, said, "That perfume was worth a year's wages. It should have been sold and the money given to the poor." Not that he cared for the poor—he was a thief, and since he was in charge of the disciples' money, he often stole some for himself.

Jesus replied, "Leave her alone. She did this in preparation for my burial. You will always have the poor among you, but you will not always have me." (John 12:1-8)

What can we learn about this event from these two accounts?

| | |
|---|---|
| Where was this gathering? | |
| Who was there? | |

| When did this happen? | |
|---|---|
| What were they doing? | |
| What's interesting about the anointing oil? | |

Do we stop here, though, with just a list of the details? Let's think about what these pieces can contribute to our deeper understanding of what happened.

Mary did *what* she could—a daring act in front of friends and family. When you live loved, your "what" matters. Though Simon could have been just another follower of Jesus, he is more likely the elderly—and healed—father of Mary, Martha, and Lazarus. According to John 12:4-6, the criticizing voice comes from Judas Iscariot, who, known to have been greedy and a thief, helped himself to what was in the disciples' moneybag. Other references indicate that some of the disciples were critical of the extravagance of Mary's act.[1]

Where is it safer to make a risky move—in front of friends or strangers? Strangers don't know or care whether you make a fool of yourself. Family does. You'll most likely never see strangers again, but you'll likely see family often. On the other hand, acting in front of strangers can be risky as well. Will a gesture be understood or not? We don't know if Mary discussed her actions with her family ahead of time or not. Either way, she must have anticipated some of the reaction. Mary was very comfortable being with Jesus. Even when there was work to be done to help her sister, Martha, Mary chose to sit and listen to Jesus. Mary was no stranger to criticism from her sister. Martha had complained to Jesus before. In the John passage, we again see that Martha was using her serving gifts while Mary chose to use her gift of giving.

We don't know how much time Mary and the disciples had spent together. The disciples had accompanied Jesus when he raised Lazarus from the dead. Mary as well as the disciples had most likely been present when Jesus had healed Simon's leprosy. How many other times might Simon have hosted Jesus and his disciples? Did she anticipate the critical nature of Judas and the others? Had she thought through the ramifications of her extravagance?

This event took place just before Jesus' crucifixion. Mary approached Jesus with her gift of perfume and poured it out with confidence, her gesture expressing her love for him and preparing his body for burial before his death, the broken flask foreshadowing the shards customarily left in the tomb after the body's anointing for burial.[2]

While Mary couldn't know specifically that in just a few days, Jesus would be crucified, she somehow understood better than others that death was in his future. The disciples sure didn't seem to follow the unfolding reality of what lay before Jesus, but Mary innately did. And Jesus underlined her insight with his response, "She did it to prepare me for burial." The fragrance of her oil would still be discernable during Jesus' final days. Her timing, though most likely unplanned, was appropriate. What was it that Mary sensed or knew that prompted her to act so boldly at a time when she knew she would be criticized?

Mary gave with compassion and understanding. She gave from the context of who God had made her to be and from what her relationship with him was making her. She sat at Jesus' feet, opening her soul to his teaching, his wisdom, and his love. Because she took the time to take him in, she "got" him. Over the days and months and perhaps years of their relationship, his investment combined with the core of her being to yield a rich essence of character, from which she later anointed him in a moment of his own great need. Spiritual intimacy had been formed, and in return, it formed her.[3]

Mary had spent time at Jesus' feet. She'd spent enough to irritate her sister. She'd spent enough to have a heart connection with Jesus. She may not have been able to predict exactly what was coming, but she knew there was something afoot. Mary knew enough to know his anointing was needed. She also knew enough about Jesus to know what would be meaningful. She knew he needed more than a prayer or a hug or a warm glance of encouragement. Mary also knew Jesus well enough to understand that her gift would be received and accepted by him. She may or may not have known what the reaction would be of the others in the room. But, because she was in relationship with Jesus, she knew that Jesus would receive her action as a gesture from her heart. That was enough to give her the courage to step forward and present her gift.

Mary was living loved. Because she had received love, she gave it. She understood what, so far, the disciples had missed. In this act of worship, she *lived* loved.[4]

Mary had received Jesus' love. She knew she had to give back. She wanted to give something that was meaningful and appropriate. Mary probably had other choices: something for Jesus' continued trip to Jerusalem, making sure the chores were done before he got there, a note about her gratitude, something she'd made. Mary chose first to accept the love of Jesus. That's the main way we return God's love. There's really no greater way to love God back for his gift of Jesus. When we accept Jesus' love, it changes us and then we live differently. Mary exemplifies this. She accepted Jesus' love, and it changed her. She took time to sit at his feet and listen. She had listened enough to know what was ahead for Jesus and what would encourage him as he prepared.

When you're loved, it's easy to come up with a list of things you want to do for those who love you. Those who are loved are able to return love in meaningful ways. Mary's gift was a testament to the love she'd received. It rose up out of the context of her relationship with Jesus. After all, a relationship with Jesus results in a response. Mary did *what* she could. And when you live loved, your "what" matters.

## CONTEMPLATE THIS

1. What do you think Mary was thinking and feeling as she walked into the room with her nard?

2. What do you think Mary was feeling as she poured her oil on Jesus?

3. Do you think Mary noticed what anyone else was doing while she made her offering?

4. What do you think mattered most to Mary as she offered her gift of nard?

5. How much of the significance of her actions do you think Mary was aware of?

6. What might it have been like to know Jesus as Mary did?

7. What do you think Martha's reaction might have been to this event?

## INVESTIGATE THIS

There is another similar account in Luke 7:36-50, but this story is not about Mary of Bethany at all. This took place at another time and place—and with different characters—but is often confused as the same account. Take a look at this account to see what is similar and different, and note the Scripture references.

| | |
|---|---|
| What are the differences between the two hosts? | |
| What are the differences between Mary and the woman in this account? | |
| What are the differences between the motives of the two women? | |
| What are the differences between Jesus' responses? | |
| What are the similarities between the two hosts? | |
| What are the similarities between Mary and the woman in this account? | |
| What are the similarities between the motives of the two women? | |
| What are the similarities between Jesus' responses? | |

8. How did each woman live out of the context of her relationship with Jesus?

9. How did each woman live loved?

## RESPOND TO THIS

Visit the SDWSC website (www.sdwsc.com) to read Ann's story.

10. What would be a comparable gathering in today's world?

11. What would it be like to be a guest at such a gathering if Jesus were there?

12. Would you risk giving Jesus a gift (large or small) at such a gathering?

13. Might God be inviting you to take a risk as an offering to him? How?

14. How are you like or unlike Mary?

15. What would it look like for you to give out of the context of your relationship with Jesus?

16. How might you love Jesus *back* by doing what you could?

17. How can you grow this week in your SDWSC abilities?

18. How can being a SDWSC person help you grow in your relationship with Jesus?

End your time by praying for opportunities in the coming week to seize SDWSC moments.

## APPLY THIS

Using an index card, create a reminder for this week to put on a desktop, dashboard, fridge, etc. On one side write the letters "SDWSC." The other side should say, "Live loved!"

Commit to keeping the card in sight all week and bringing a story, written on an index card, to the next session.

Consider also posting your story on the SDWSC website (www .sdwsc.com).

Name

Date

My SDWSC Story

# What If I Did What I Could?

## How to live loved.

*"I don't have to start anything big, but [just] love others one little step at a time."*—ANN

Begin your time with the "Steve's Story" video clip from the SDWSC website (www.sdwsc.com). Share the story you wrote this past week. Explain why that story was meaningful for you. Post your story on the storyboard.

## CONSIDER THIS

In life we live out what we believe in our hearts. God loves you. The Bible tells you so. Do you believe it? Do you live as though you believe it?

Most of us don't. We've heard God's love for us preached to us from the pulpit and piped into our iPods. We've read God's love for us in greeting cards and in Scripture verses. We've prayed God's love for us over ourselves and over those we care about. But do we really believe that God loves us to the point that we *live* loved?

How much does God love me? I mean really and truly. What do I really believe about the depth of God's love for me? Is what I say different from what I feel in my heart?

I'm a woman whom God loves. What if I just start there: I am loved.

I used to think such a thing was silly, immature, unnecessary. Unworthy me? Loved by God? Humph! Shame would gurgle up in my soul against such a thought. In seconds, a "shame fest" would overtake me, quietly and in secret, and I felt like a child caught in a naughty act.[1]

What does it mean for us to take those words, "I love you," from Jesus and swallow them, digest them, and allow them to become a part of who we are? That's the beauty of Mary and what she did. She understood the depth of Jesus' love. She knew it enough to trust Jesus as she took a risk. She knew it enough to want to give back.

Consider 1 John 4:7-12 and what it says about God's love for us:

Dear friends, let us continue to love one another, for love comes from God. Anyone who loves is a child of God and knows God. But anyone who does not love does not know God, for God is love.

God showed how much he loved us by sending his one and only Son into the world so that we might have eternal life through him. This is real love—not that we loved God, but that he loved us and sent his Son as a sacrifice to take away our sins.

Dear friends, since God loved us that much, we surely ought to love each other. No one has ever seen God. But if we love each other, God lives in us, and his love is brought to full expression in us.

Use this chart to help think through what this verse is saying. Note the answers below with the Scripture references.

| | |
|---|---|
| Where does love come from? | |
| How do we know that God loves us? | |
| What do we do to receive God's love? | |
| How does God show his love for us in the world? | |
| What are we supposed to do with God's love? | |

Now read verse 19: "We love each other because he loved us first." God loved us first! Before we were born, before we messed up, before we knew we needed his love, God sent Jesus to show us how much he loves us. No matter what, God loves you. Chewing on that, swallowing it, digesting it, making it fully part of your being takes a lifetime. We can all begin each day taking a new taste of God's love. Savoring this love is living loved. That's what Mary did. You and I can do it too.

Mary's action shifts me away from my shame. It's not that I deserve to be loved. I don't. She didn't. No one really does. It's just that Jesus loves me. It's a fact. When I realize I'm not so darling in and of myself—and that I don't have to be—but am still irrevocably loved and valued and created for good, his love becomes all the more stunning to me.[2]

Can you accept God's love for you? I once received a challenge: Spend ten minutes every day focusing on God's love for you. Really? At first the challenge rang hollow, but I decided to give it a try. For the first few days, I almost forgot. You know, I zipped through my days and suddenly remembered the challenge mid-task. So I'd stop and think about God's love, and after about thirty seconds, I lost concentration and was making a grocery list again. On about the fourth day though, just when I stopped to consider the thought that God loved me, something happened. Honest. It's as if I'd just felt God saying to me, "I love you," and then he said my name. It stunned me. I'd never heard that before: "I love you, _____."

Try it. Try ten minutes a day, focusing on this sentence: "I love you, _____," and fill in your name. You don't have to fully understand it; just take a step. Look at yourself in the mirror. That person you see is the one God sent Jesus to earth for. That person you see is the same one Jesus died for. Stunning! Try believing this thought. And then try living as though you believe this thought. That's living loved.

What might living loved look like? Mary was a pretty good example. She sat at Jesus' feet and enjoyed his presence. She didn't let the pressures of life deter her from spending time with Jesus (at least not all of the time). She trusted him enough to take risks. She knew Jesus well enough to understand what he needed.

There are some things she didn't do too. She didn't start twelve (or even one) Bible studies that we know of. She didn't sell her home and belongings to attend every appearance Jesus made. She didn't plant churches or make guest appearances at the Sanhedrin. She didn't become a nun or a martyr. Mary was Mary. She basked in Jesus' love and did what she could. That's living loved.

Living loved means that I "get" that God loves *me* and you "get" that God loves *you* and then we live out this belief in how we live by just doing what we can. It might mean sharing half my peanut butter sandwich or half my bonus. It doesn't matter. In God's eyes, the giving is the same. The half sandwich can be used to make the same eternal impact as the half bonus.

How do we know what our "what" is? How do we know the difference between one more good thing we should do and the one thing we could do that would truly make a difference? Take a look at our biblical examples. We can start small. The biblical superstars did. David was a shepherd, and so was Moses. Don't fret—you don't have to do it all perfectly. These two guys made big mistakes, and God still loved them and used them mightily as they did what they could.

Lastly, living loved means living freely and resisting our eternal self-editing that tells us that we aren't loved and can't make a difference. We can be our own worst enemy.

"Leave her alone." That's what Jesus said to the room filled with criticism. In other words, "Quit bothering her." I turn the eyes of my imagination away from Jesus and look back at Mary, seeing her the way he sees her: earnest and pure, her action in the moment beautiful.

I am struck by his command: "Leave her alone."

*Her* who?

Well, Mary, of course, but also *you*.

Dear one, leave *you* alone. Leave yourself alone. Quit bothering the *her* that is *you*. Stop needling her, judging her, messing with her, being embarrassed by her. Don't tie her up in knots and make her all anxious and sweaty. Silence the stream of self-editing that tells her that she's not enough, that she's silly or worthless, that she has really bad ideas and is way out of line. Take your hands off her. Let her be![3]

## CONTEMPLATE THIS

1. What are two concrete examples of ways that God has demonstrated his love for you? Where were you? What were you doing? How did you experience God's love?

2. How would you define living loved to a twelve-year-old?

3. Let's say you and Mary were having lunch. What two questions would you ask her?

4. What are your biggest obstacles to living loved? How do you self-edit, judge, or focus on your past mistakes and then don't live loved?

5. What gifts are easiest for you to give?

6. What do you need to stop doing?

## INVESTIGATE THIS

What does God's love for us look like? Let's look at a familiar Scripture passage, 1 Corinthians 13:4-8.

Love is patient and kind. Love is not jealous or boastful or proud or rude. It does not demand its own way. It is not irritable, and it keeps no record of being wronged. It does not rejoice about injustice but rejoices whenever the truth wins out. Love never gives up, never loses faith, is always hopeful, and endures through every circumstance.

Prophecy and speaking in unknown languages and special knowledge will become useless. But love will last forever!

This description is as much about how God loves us as it is about how we can love others.

Use this passage to answer the following questions about what is and isn't love.

| What is love? | What isn't love? |
|---|---|
|  |  |

7. What does this say about how God loves you?

8. What are some things God doesn't do because of his love for you?

9. What difference does God's love make?

## RESPOND TO THIS

Visit the SDWSC website (www.sdwsc.com) to read Linda's story.

10. How do you receive God's love?

11. How can you be more open to God's love?

12. How does living loved help us with SDWSC living?

13. Where does SDWSC living originate?

14. Who is someone you know who lives loved well?

15. What defines a person who lives loved?

16. How will you know when you're living loved?

End your time by praying for opportunities in the coming week to seize SDWSC moments.

## APPLY THIS

Using an index card, create a reminder for this week to put on a desktop, dashboard, fridge, etc. On one side write the letters "SDWSC." The other side should say, "I love you, _____. Signed, God."

Commit to keeping the card in sight all week and bringing a story, written on an index card, to the next session.

Consider also posting your story on the SDWSC website (www.sdwsc.com).

Name

Date

My SDWSC Story

LESSON FOUR

# What If I Didn't Do What I Could?

## Live with no regrets.

*"The phrase 'She did what she could' is set
in my mind and in my heart . . .
it has freed me in so many ways . . . to do things
I've never done and to not do things
without feeling guilty."*—NICOLE

B egin your time with "Heather's Story Part 2" from the SDWSC website (www.sdwsc.com). Share the story you wrote this past week. Explain why that story was meaningful for you. Post your story on the storyboard.

## CONSIDER THIS

Peter, the "rock" on which Jesus declared he would build his church (see Matthew 16:18), and the only one brave enough to get out of the boat to walk to Jesus on the water, was undoubtedly a disciple who loved and trusted Jesus. But did he live without regrets? Take a look at what Matthew 26:37-46 says:

> He took Peter and Zebedee's two sons, James and John, and he became anguished and distressed. He told them, "My soul is crushed with grief to the point of death. Stay here and keep watch with me."
>
> He went on a little farther and bowed with his face to the ground, praying, "My Father! If it is possible, let this cup of suffering be taken away from me. Yet I want your will to be done, not mine."
>
> Then he returned to the disciples and found them asleep. He said to Peter, "Couldn't you watch with me even one hour? Keep watch and pray, so that you will not give in to temptation. For the spirit is willing, but the body is weak!"
>
> Then Jesus left them a second time and prayed, "My Father! If this cup cannot be taken away unless I drink it, your will be done." When he returned to them again, he found them sleeping, for they couldn't keep their eyes open.
>
> So he went to pray a third time, saying the same things again. Then he came to the disciples and said, "Go ahead and

sleep. Have your rest. But look — the time has come. The Son of Man is betrayed into the hands of sinners. Up, let's be going. Look, my betrayer is here!"

Jesus had one request of his closest followers: Please pray for me. And what did Peter, James, and John do? They took naps. Not once, but three times in a row. Notice that Jesus addressed Peter specifically. Pray, please. Peter didn't. He rested instead. What difference might prayer have made? Would Peter still have lopped off the guard's ear? Would he still have denied his relationship with Jesus three times? There's no way to know.

What if you didn't do what you could? Ugh. Here comes the guilt. There are so very many "she didn't do what she could" stories, in my life and in yours. They point the finger of accusation at us, and we squirm in discomfort.[1] There is one comforting reality though: I'm in good company. I have a long "didn't do" list. I didn't pray either — for my friend, my daughter, my husband, my mother. They all asked or I volunteered. But then I forgot or got busy or tired. I can think of plenty of other "didn't dos," too. Most were little things; a few were big.

When my kids were young, we visited a grandma who couldn't get out much and spent much of her time alone. We started well and then got busy and let more time pass between visits. One week my daughter repeatedly asked to visit our friend. I was too busy doing other good things. At week's end, we received word that our friend had passed away. More than twenty years later, I still regret missing our visit. I wish life had a rewind button.

What if Mary "didn't"? What if she hadn't opened her jar of nard? What if, to avoid an awkward situation, she chose to anoint Jesus later — in private — when the disciples were off doing something else? What if she decided to wait until Jesus came back after the Passover?

Jesus would still have done what he came to do. But would he have been affirmed and encouraged uniquely by Mary living loved before him, first receiving and then returning his love? If Mary had anointed him when only a few others were present, would it have been recorded? Would it have meant as much to Jesus? Would he have pronounced her action "a beautiful thing"? Would it have been an example of anything to us? Waiting a week would mean that the opportunity was lost. Fortunately, Mary did what she could when it was needed.

Does Jesus really need you and me? Will he send someone else if we "don't"? When the priest and the Levite didn't, there was the Good Samaritan. When everyone else chose otherwise, Noah chose to listen and obey. When the other sisters went home, Ruth stuck with Naomi. If Mary hadn't, would someone else have stepped in?

These questions will be answered over a cup of tea (or something better) in eternity. For now, what do I do? What if I didn't take the easy road of allowing everyone else around me to invest? What if I didn't excuse my own lack of action with the rationalization that what I could have done and didn't was really unnecessary, repetitive, or unvalued anyway? *They have enough canned food. Nobody will notice if I don't volunteer in my child's class this year. My twenty-five dollars won't make a dent.* What if instead of waiting to be invited, I jumped in, took the initiative, volunteered, offered my two widow's mites?[2]

If I did what I could, I would be acting out of God's love for me in a given moment when he has more for me to experience. More because I move beyond considering to engaging. More because I invest out of an attitude of caring rather than out of a sense of obligation. More because I act instead of letting someone else act. More because I initiate, knowing that because I am, I can do.

More because I do instead of don't.[3]

I'm not going to get it right all of the time. Neither are you. We're not called to live a life of guilt; we're called to live loved. When I live loved, I soak in all that God has for me as often as I can.

Welcome to the club. We all blow it. SDWSC is not about guilt avoidance. It's not about paying it forward or doing random acts of kindness or living a better life. It's not about obedience just for the sake of obedience. When I'm filled, I want to give others what I have. When I miss an opportunity, I return to God and receive his grace and mercy. I choose to spend less time on remorse, which gives me more time for giving. This is living a life with no regrets. It sounds simple, but it's not. We know better. But we can keep trying.

## CONTEMPLATE THIS

1. What are some times when you wished someone would have done something (anything) and then didn't?

2. Would it have mattered to you if someone had done something for you that wasn't perfect rather than done nothing?

3. Think of a time when you didn't do something. How do you feel about it?

4. What are the consequences when we don't do what we could?

5. What difference does it really make whether we do something or not?

6. Do you think God will always find someone else to do what we didn't? Why or why not?

7. What are some other biblical examples of those who didn't do what they could?

8. What was the consequence of their inaction?

9. What should be our reason for doing something for someone else?

## INVESTIGATE THIS

Read 1 John 4:17-21.

And as we live in God, our love grows more perfect. So we will not be afraid on the day of judgment, but we can face him with confidence because we live like Jesus here in this world.

Such love has no fear, because perfect love expels all fear. If we are afraid, it is for fear of punishment, and this shows that we have not fully experienced his perfect love. We love each other because he loved us first.

If someone says, "I love God," but hates a Christian brother or sister, that person is a liar; for if we don't love people we can see, how can we love God, whom we cannot see? And he has given us this command: Those who love God must also love their Christian brothers and sisters.

Answer the following questions, noting the Scripture references.

| What contributes to SDWSC living? | What detracts from SDWSC living? |
|---|---|
|  |  |

10. What fears get in our way of doing what we can?

11. How can we find more of God's love?

12. What obstacles, fears, and inadequacies contribute to your "didn't do" list?

13. What is one fear you can confess and ask for God's help in overcoming through his love?

14. What can you do that no one has ever invited you to do?

## RESPOND TO THIS

Read "Nickie's Story" from the SDWSC website (www.sdwsc.com).

15. How does Nickie's story help us see what we don't need to do?

16. What are some things you can do to help yourself avoid "didn't do" situations?

17. What can we do when we commit a "didn't do"?

18. How can we work toward a life of no regrets?

End your time by praying for opportunities in the coming week to seize SDWSC moments.

## APPLY THIS

Using an index card, create a reminder for this week to put on a desktop, dashboard, fridge, etc. On one side write the letters "SDWSC." The other side should say, "Live with no regrets."

Commit to keeping the card in sight all week and bringing a story, written on an index card, to the next session.

Consider also posting your story on the SDWSC website (www.sdwsc.com).

Name

Date

My SDWSC Story

# What If We Did What We Could?

## You plus me equals we.

*"I called my husband on the way home and he was so accepting of the fact that I'd just given our dinner away. He returned my question by asking, 'So how can I help you?' He picked up pizza on his way home from work, and we pulled in the driveway at the same time. He was smiling because we had done what we could!"*—HEATHER

Open with the "Karen's Story" video clip from the SDWSC website (www.sdwsc.com). Share the story you wrote this past week. Explain why that story was meaningful for you. Post your story on the storyboard.

## CONSIDER THIS

You plus me equals we. There's power in numbers. Yet often the "we" doesn't happen because someone is dis-included. Let's return to Mark 14:3-9 and see what almost happened to Mary:

> While he was in Bethany, reclining at the table in the home of Simon the Leper, a woman came with an alabaster jar of very expensive perfume, made of pure nard. She broke the jar and poured the perfume on his head.
>
> Some of those present were saying indignantly to one another, "Why this waste of perfume? It could have been sold for more than a year's wages and the money given to the poor." And they rebuked her harshly.
>
> "Leave her alone," said Jesus. "Why are you bothering her? She has done a beautiful thing to me. The poor you will always have with you, and you can help them any time you want. But you will not always have me. She did what she could. She poured perfume on my body beforehand to prepare for my burial. Truly I tell you, wherever the gospel is preached throughout the world, what she has done will also be told, in memory of her." (NIV)

Have you ever run into people who demand that you believe everything the way they believe it or you can't be part of their "we"? Have you ever experienced what it feels like to be excluded from the great Christian "we"?

Mary nearly was. A roomful of followers collectively gasped at her action and then troubled her to the point of rejection. If the folks at that dinner party had had their way, Mary would never have acted at all, her gift of anointing Jesus' body before his death scuttled before it could even get away from the dock. But Jesus interceded. He pronounced her action beautiful and paired it with the preaching of the good news for all time.[1]

Mary was almost dis-included. It happens. We get started on our SDWSC journey and are blindsided by naysayers: "There are starving people in Africa who need things—and deserve them—way more." "How can you rationalize spending so much time with her?" "Why are you praying instead of doing?" (Or *doing* instead of *praying*?)

If it's not the naysayers; it's those with opposing points of view. If you're focusing on marriages, you'll be criticized for not helping single parents. If you're focusing on kids, you'll be criticized for not challenging the root of the problem. If you're focusing on the political system, you'll be criticized for socializing with the wrong folks. If you're collecting for the latest natural disaster, you'll be criticized for not caring for the poor up the street.

You can probably add several more jabs—or downright opposition—just in the time since you began working your way through this study. It's easy to start thinking we're working alone. We can feel we're dragging others up our hill—on our own, in our own strength. Weariness sets in quickly.

What might happen if we turned and looked over our shoulders? How many people have our backs? Our hearts? Our spouses or our coworkers may not *always* agree with our SDWSC choices, but most of the time they're filling in for us somewhere, somehow. Our kids are learning from our example and most likely helping us. Our parents often provide childcare and a listening ear. Our friends encourage, help bring food, or take our kids. Our Bible study group prays. Or maybe you're one of the people who has someone else's back, helping them with childcare, errands, or housecleaning while they help someone else.

What might happen if we look beyond what we're doing? What if we listen to the success stories of those around us? When we listen to others who are making a difference, we're energized. We cry, we smile, we understand the victory, we rejoice. We see the bigger picture.

What if we did what we could?

We can look at the mountain ahead and become overwhelmed. Or we can look over our shoulders and see all those who are helping us, working alongside us, making positive changes in all kinds of places. You plus me equals we. There is strength in numbers. Stop, look, and rejoice in those who have joined you. Stop, look, and rejoice in those who haven't joined *you* but have joined God in another effort that matters just as much at the one you've selected.

It's vital that each one of us do what *we* individually could. It is also vital that *we* do what *we* could together and that we respect how others do what they could so that *we* are all doing what *we* could. We don't have to be the same to be *we*. We don't have to agree with each other's finer points of theology to serve a meal to the hungry. In fact, in many cases we will have less impact if we all do the same thing than we would if we each did what we could alone and then all our efforts were added to a communal *we*.[2]

We can vote someone off the island or we can encourage each other the way we need encouragement. We can be a strong we. We can make a difference in a million different ways if we respect and encourage each other's efforts. There is so much to do. Our individual budgets are limited. We all have only twenty-four hours in a day. But together we have so much.

What could we *all* accomplish if each one of us did what she could and then *we* added all these efforts together? This is the body of

Christ in action, uniquely called to both an individual and a corporate investment of who *we* are.[3]

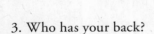

1. Have you ever been dis-included?

2. Have you ever dis-included someone else?

3. Who has your back?

4. Whose back do you have?

5. Who needs you to have her back but you are resisting?

6. What effect does dis-including someone from her calling have on the bigger picture of the world's needs?

7. How could "We did what we could" thinking help accomplish more than just "I did what I could" thinking?

8. How are you involved in "We did what we could" thinking?

## INVESTIGATE THIS

Read 1 Corinthians 12:12-27.

The human body has many parts, but the many parts make up one whole body. So it is with the body of Christ. Some of us are Jews, some are Gentiles, some are slaves, and some are free. But we have all been baptized into one body by one Spirit, and we all share the same Spirit.

Yes, the body has many different parts, not just one part. If the foot says, "I am not a part of the body because I am not a hand," that does not make it any less a part of the body. And if the ear says, "I am not part of the body because I am not an eye," would that make it any less a part of the body? If the whole body were an eye, how would you hear? Or if your whole body were an ear, how would you smell anything?

But our bodies have many parts, and God has put each part just where he wants it. How strange a body would be if it had only one part! Yes, there are many parts, but only one body. The eye can never say to the hand, "I don't need you." The head can't say to the feet, "I don't need you."

In fact, some parts of the body that seem weakest and least important are actually the most necessary. And the parts we regard as less honorable are those we clothe with the greatest care. So we carefully protect those parts that should not be seen, while the more honorable parts do not require this special care. So God has put the body together such that extra honor and care are given to those parts that have less dignity. This makes for harmony among the members, so that all the members care for each other. If one part suffers, all the parts suffer with it, and if one part is honored, all the parts are glad.

All of you together are Christ's body, and each of you is a part of it.

Answer the following questions with biblical references.

| How are we to be like a body? | |
|---|---|

| Why aren't we all the same body part? | |
|---|---|
| How should we treat the other body parts? | |
| What happens to our part of the body if another part is not functioning well? | |
| How does Christ view the different parts of the body? | |
| Whose choice is it to be a particular body part? | |

9. How does God desire to include all in his body?

10. Who shares your part of Christ's body?

11. How should we treat a body part that we don't agree with?

12. How do we work toward body health?

13. How does "We did what we could" thinking help foster body health?

## RESPOND TO THIS

Read "Heather's Story Part 1" from the SDWSC website (www.sdwsc .com).

14. How can your family participate in SDWSC living?

15. How do you include and recognize others who are covering your back?

16. How have the times when you were dis-included shaped you?

17. How can we help each other overcome the tendency to judge others' intentions and projects?

End your time by praying for opportunities in the coming week to seize SDWSC moments.

## APPLY THIS

Using an index card, create a reminder for this week to put on a desktop, dashboard, fridge, etc. On one side write the letters "SDWSC." The other side should say, "You plus me equals we."

Commit to keeping the card in sight all week and bringing a story, written on an index card, to the next session.

Consider also posting your story on the SDWSC website (www.sdwsc.com).


Name

Date

My SDWSC Story

# What If We All Did What We Could?

## The power of "we."

*"My MOPS group knew they couldn't take away my pain from losing [my son] Ethan, but they 'did what they could' by bringing us meals, praying for us, collecting baby clothes for Grant, mowing our lawn, and so on. The group is truly a gift from God."*—REBECCA

B egin with the opening video from the "Your SDWSC Stories" clip on the SDWSC website (www.sdwsc.com). Share the story you wrote this past week. Explain why that story was meaningful for you. Post your story on the storyboard.

## CONSIDER THIS

Our final words to someone are often the ones we feel are most important. If you've ever sat at the bedside of someone who is dying, you know the urgency of their words. Jesus asked his disciples to meet him just before ascending to heaven, and this is what he told them:

> I have been given all authority in heaven and on earth. Therefore, go and make disciples of all the nations, baptizing them in the name of the Father and the Son and the Holy Spirit. Teaching these new disciples to obey all the commands I have given you. And be sure of this: I am with you always, even to the end of the age. (Matthew 28:18-20)

How do we go into all the nations, make disciples, and teach them how to obey what Jesus commanded? One SDWSC choice at a time. It could be with a purchased pizza, an adoption, a donation of used clothes, an encouraging word, or helping someone find the life-giving love of Jesus. It could be with hundreds of hours at a local charity, teaching a weekly Bible study, becoming a missionary, or the founding of a nonprofit. All get equal kudos from God. All are equally needed.

Individually, each action is a small drop in the bucket of worldwide needs, but collectively they fill the bucket. The power of "we" is amazing. I can't cure depression or world hunger, but I can call a friend who is feeling down and send five dollars to a relief organization. If I were the only one who did this, my two mites would still matter, but they would matter more if they were multiplied by the mites of others. When others in my small group also make a phone call and send five dollars, the effect grows. Think of the others in your community who do the same. Multiply that by the number of communities in your state, in this country. Expand your thinking to those around the world who give. It's mind-boggling. It's something only God can see or orchestrate.

When we see that we're just one person among millions, when we see that we're just one part of something too big for us to comprehend—that's freeing. While my "what" matters, I don't have to do it all. I just need to do my part. I'm a part of a huge, powerful "we." I'm needed to do my part. I'm loved in spite of what I do or don't do. And so is everyone else. God chose me to do my important part. God chose you to do your important part.

You plus me equals "we," and there's great power in "we"! Can we embrace the power? We don't have to hold the same exact view of parenting to reach out and offer to unstick the plumbing in a single mom's home. We can build a well in Africa alongside those who believe that Communion should be served only by a priest. And by the way, those who receive will be blessed and want to know more. They will want to discover the source of the love we share. Those who are enlisted to help will see the love of Christ demonstrated in words and deeds. All of them could become part of the "we."

What could we all accomplish if each one of us did what he or she could? I might minister to moms. You might stand against abuse. He feeds the hungry. She works for justice. They advocate for the homeless. Together we might change the world. Many acts. One "we."[1]

Some kneel in the end zone with a prayer of gratitude. Some gather their troops for a prayer of thanksgiving. Some wear a cross. Some sing worship songs while they work. Some pick up runny-nosed kids and wipe their tears while explaining God's love. Some start grassroots organizations with Christian names. Some lead Bible studies in or behind bars. The one thing they all have in common is that they're serving out of the love with which they've been filled. It's our relationship with Jesus that speaks loud and clear. It flows through our actions and our words. And when our relationship intertwines with others, it becomes a message that can't be missed. It's not a resounding gong or clanging cymbal; it's a glorious melody that both inspires and leads to the love of Jesus and then to the nations of the world.

She did what she could. One girl entered a relationship with Jesus, and because a relationship with Jesus results in a response, she did what she could. She lived loved. Jesus invites us to do the same. He beckons us to a relationship with him, a relationship that results in a response, an action. Going. Doing. Giving. Loving. When we know Jesus and are known by him, we can live loved—all of us. Individually and together. You. And me. *We*.

What if *we* did what *we* could?[2]

## CONTEMPLATE THIS

1. How is God's love revealed in your SDWSC actions?

2. How could you include others in your SDWSC actions?

3. Who in your circle of influence has heard the good news as a result of your SDWSC actions?

4. When have you seen a small piece of the power of "we" in action?

5. Who do you know who needs to hear the good news through an SDWSC choice?

6. How does Jesus' love naturally flow through you?

7. What's the most inspiring SDWSC story you've heard? Why is it so inspiring to you?

## INVESTIGATE THIS

Read 1 Peter 3:13-18 and think about the hope that is within you:

> Who will want to harm you if you are eager to do good? But even if you suffer for doing what is right, God will reward you for it. So don't worry or be afraid of their threats. Instead, you must worship Christ as Lord of your life. And if someone asks about your Christian hope, always be ready to explain it. But do this in a gentle and respectful way. Keep your conscience clear. Then if people speak against you, they will be ashamed when they see what a good life you live because you belong to Christ. Remember, it is better to suffer for doing good, if that is what God wants, than to suffer for doing wrong!
>
> Christ suffered for our sins once for all time. He never sinned, but he died for sinners to bring you safely home to God. He suffered physical death, but he was raised to life in the Spirit.

Look through the passage for the answers to each of the following questions.

| | |
|---|---|
| What should you always be prepared for? | |
| What is there to fear? | |
| What is it best to suffer for? | |

| How are we to give our testimonies? | |
|---|---|
| Why should we be ready to give a testimony? | |

8. What is your source of hope?

9. When others ask you about your source of hope, what do you say?

10. What do you fear when it comes to sharing your testimony?

11. How does your hope help fuel the power of "we"?

## RESPOND TO THIS

Read "Rebecca's Story" from the SDWSC website (www.sdwsc.com).

12. How can you share SDWSC with someone else this week?

13. What has been the most important lesson you've learned from this SDWSC study?

14. How has SDWSC thinking helped you with your testimony?

End your time by praying for opportunities in the coming week to seize SDWSC moments.

## APPLY THIS

Using an index card, create a reminder for this week to put on a desktop, dashboard, fridge, etc. On one side write the letters "SDWSC." The other side should say, "What if we did what we could?"

Commit to keeping the card in sight all week.

Consider posting your story on the SDWSC website (www .sdwsc.com).

Name

Date

My SDWSC Story

# Notes

Lesson One: She Did What She Could
1. Elisa Morgan, *She Did What She Could* (Wheaton, IL: Tyndale, 2009), 6.
2. Morgan, 9.
3. Morgan, 17.
4. Morgan, 19.
5. Morgan, 29.

Lesson Two: Who Did What She Could and Why?
1. Elisa Morgan, *She Did What She Could* (Wheaton, IL: Tyndale, 2009), 4.
2. William Barclay, *The Gospel of Mark* (Philadelphia: Westminster, 1975), 326.
3. Morgan, 23.
4. Morgan, 23.

Lesson Three: What If I Did What I Could?
1. Elisa Morgan, *She Did What She Could* (Wheaton, IL: Tyndale, 2009), 41.
2. Morgan, 41.
3. Morgan, 73–74.

Lesson Four: What If I Didn't Do What I Could?

1. Elisa Morgan, *She Did What She Could* (Wheaton, IL: Tyndale, 2009), 51.
2. Morgan, 49.
3. Morgan, 53.

Lesson Five: What If We Did What We Could?

1. Elisa Morgan, *She Did What She Could* (Wheaton, IL: Tyndale, 2009), 91–92.
2. Morgan, 96.
3. Morgan, 90.

Lesson Six: What If We All Did What We Could?

1. Elisa Morgan, *She Did What She Could* (Wheaton, IL: Tyndale, 2009), 96.
2. Morgan, 97.

# About the Author

ELISA MORGAN is the publisher of *FullFill*, a digital magazine for women of all ages and stages (www.fullfill.org).

For twenty years, Elisa served as CEO of MOPS International (www.mops.org). Under her leadership, MOPS grew from 350 to more than 4,000 groups throughout the United States and in 30 other countries, impacting more than 100,000 moms every year. Elisa now serves as President Emerita.

Elisa received a BS from the University of Texas and an MDiv from Denver Seminary. She served as the dean of women of Western Bible College (now Colorado Christian University) and on the board of ECFA (Evangelical Council for Financial Accountability). She is married to Evan and has two grown children and one grandchild who live near her in Centennial, Colorado.

You're surrounded by needs.
Where do you start?

How do you start?

Five words that will change your life!

ISBN 978-1-4143-3378-6

**SHE DID WHAT SHE COULD™** — Jesus said these words about Mary after she anointed him with oil. SDWSC — "She did what she could." Not everything, not more than most, just, simply, what she could. And Jesus loved her for it. What if we lived our faith that way? What if we responded to the need before us — in the moment — with an everyday action? In the front yard, at the market, on an airplane. **Elisa Morgan guides you to ways to begin serving right where you are.**

Find a supplier at tyndale.com

Where does your voice fit?
Text REFILL to 22828 and sign up NOW!
Welcome to
FullFill™
For women. For leaders. Online. Anytime.
A digital magazine complete with compelling articles, beautiful images and inspirational videos from Elisa Morgan.
FullFill™.org — created for women like you who are living out your influence to impact your world.
We speak your language! www.FullFill.org